D1518836

My First Animal Library

Bats

by Martha E. H. Rustad

Bullfrog
Books

Ideas for Parents and Teachers

Bullfrog Books let children practice reading informational texts at the earliest reading levels. Repetition, familiar words, and photo labels support early readers.

Before Reading

- Discuss the cover photo. What does it tell them?
- Look at the picture glossary together. Read and discuss the words.

Read the Book

- "Walk" through the book and look at the photos. Let the child ask questions. Point out the photo labels.
- Read the book to the child, or have him or her read independently.

After Reading

- Prompt the child to think more. Ask: Have you ever seen a bat? What other animals does it look like? How can bats help people?

Bullfrog Books are published by Jump!
5357 Penn Avenue South
Minneapolis, MN 55419
www.jumplibrary.com

Rustad, Martha E. H. (Martha Elizabeth Hillman), 1975-
  Bats / by Martha E.H. Rustad.
    p. cm. -- (Bullfrog books. My first animal library, nocturnal animals)
  Summary: "This easy-to-read nonfiction story tells a "night in the life" of a bat, from waking up, finding food, and taking care of babies, to going back to sleep when the sun comes up"-- Provided by publisher.
  Audience: 005.
  Audience: K to grade 3.
  Includes bibliographical references and index.
  ISBN 978-1-62031-068-7 (hardcover) -- ISBN 978-1-62496-068-0 (ebook)
  1. Bats--Juvenile literature. I. Title.
  QL737.C5R87 2014
  599.4--dc23
                                    2013004604

Editor Rebecca Glaser
Series Designer Ellen Huber
Book Designer Danny Nanos
Book Production Sean Melom

Photo Credits: All photos by Shutterstock

Printed in the United States at Corporate Graphics in North Mankato, Minnesota.
5-2013 / PO 1003
10 9 8 7 6 5 4 3 2 1

Bats at Night

The sun sets.
Night begins.
Bats wake up.

5

Bats are hungry.

They fly.

They look for food.

Bats catch bugs in the air.

Some bats eat fruit.

**Bats use sound to find food.
Bats cry out.**

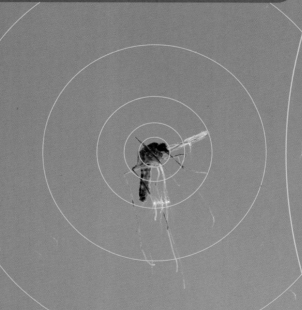

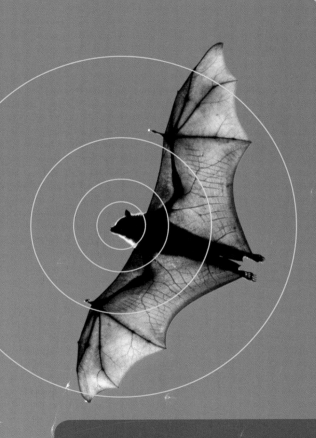

They listen for an echo.
Echoes bounce off food.

11

pup

Baby bats cannot fly.
The pups wait.

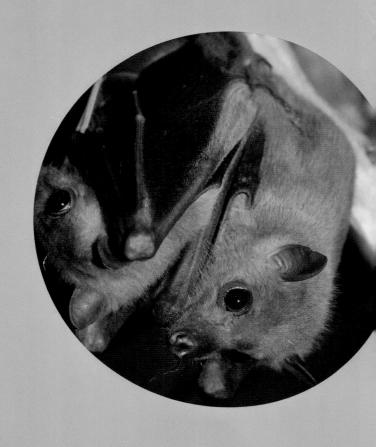

13

The bats are done eating.
They fly back to the cave.

Mother bats feed the pups milk.

Bats roost.

They hang upside down.

Father bats hang in one spot.

Mother bats and pups hang in another.

The cave is safe and cool.

The bat colony is hidden.

Snakes and owls cannot find them.

The sun rises.
Day begins.
Bats go to sleep.

Parts of a Bat

wings
Bats are the only mammals that can fly.

ears
Bats often have big ears. They can hear well.

fingers
A bat's fingers are part of its wings.

claws
Bats' claws let them hang upside down.

fur
Bats are mammals.

Picture Glossary

colony
A group that lives together.

pup
A baby bat.

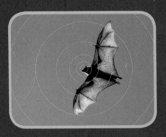

echo
A sound that reflects back from an object to a listener.

roost
To gather as a group to rest.

Index

To Learn More

Learning more is as easy as 1, 2, 3.

1) Go to www.factsurfer.com

2) Enter "bats" into the search box.

3) Click the "Surf" button to see a list of websites.

With factsurfer.com, finding more information is just a click away.